GW01159122

The Golden Compass

In the sky where stars collide,
A beacon bright, our hearts will guide.
Through shadows deep and winds that wail,
The compass points where dreams prevail.

With every step, our hopes align,
Across the seas, through sands that shine.
Adventures call, the brave shall rise,
With every turn, we claim the skies.

A Dance with Destiny

Beneath the moon's enchanting glow,
Two souls entwined, their fate in flow.
A whispered tune, a gentle sway,
In perfect rhythm, night turns to day.

With every heartbeat, time stands still,
In every glance, a secret thrill.
Together they weave a timeless song,
A dance with destiny, where they belong.

The Seeds of Tomorrow

In fertile ground, a vision sown,
With tender care, our dreams are grown.
Each seed a story, waiting to bloom,
In sunlight's grace, dispelling gloom.

With patience strong, we tend the field,
To future's harvest, our hearts will yield.
Hope takes root in the soil of time,
A promise whispered in nature's rhyme.

Labyrinth of Longing

Within the maze, our whispers trace,
The paths of heart in a timeless space.
Lost yet seeking, we wander wide,
Through twists and turns where dreams confide.

Each corner holds a silent plea,
A glimpse of what we long to see.
Through tangled threads of joy and pain,
We'll find our way, our hearts sustain.

Wings of a Thousand Visions

In dreams where visions soar high,
I chase the clouds that drift by.
Each thought a feather, light and free,
A tapestry of what could be.

Through valleys deep and mountains wide,
I find the strength I hold inside.
With every step, my spirit sings,
Embracing life on hopeful wings.

Crafting My Tomorrow

With every choice, a path I lay,
In fields of gold, I find my way.
Threads of dreams in colors bright,
I weave my future, purest light.

The clay of fate is soft and warm,
In hands of hope, I shape my form.
With patience, passion, heart aglow,
I mold the seeds of what will grow.

Beyond the Horizon of Hopes

Where sky meets ocean, dreams arise,
A distant land beneath the skies.
Across the waves, I hear the call,
To journey forth, to risk it all.

In whispers soft, the future sings,
Awakening the hope it brings.
With every step, my heart will soar,
Beyond the horizon, evermore.

Echoes of a Bright Future

In the quiet, I hear the sound,
Of dreams that rise from underground.
With every echo, hope takes flight,
A symphony of pure delight.

The path ahead is paved with light,
Guiding me through the darkest night.
With courage bold, I will pursue,
The echoes whispered, bright and true.

The Alchemy of Calling

In whispers soft, our dreams take flight,
They blend and twist, a dance of light.
A path unknown, where shadows play,
We follow hearts, lead us away.

With every turn, the echoes ring,
Each step we take, a new beginning.
Transform the pain, embrace the fight,
In alchemy, we find our might.

Unwritten Chapters of Life

A book awaits, both blank and bright,
With ink of joy, and shades of night.
Each moment ticks, we write our tale,
Through storms we rise, through winds we sail.

The pages turn, a story flows,
A dance of fate, where wisdom grows.
In every line, a chance to see,
The unwritten fate, awaits for me.

The Seeds of Tomorrow's Flourish

In quiet soil, we plant the dreams,
Where hope takes root, in sunlight's beams.
Each seed we sow, a vision's rise,
From gentle hands, the future flies.

With care we nurture, through joy and strife,
In every tear, a pulse of life.
The blossoms wait, in colors bold,
Tomorrow's story, yet untold.

Melodies of Uncharted Waters

Beneath the waves, where secrets hide,
A song emerges, the ocean's guide.
With every splash, a tale unfolds,
Of journeys sought, and treasures bold.

The winds carry notes, both low and high,
As dreams take flight, beneath the sky.
In rhythms deep, we find our way,
Through uncharted waters, come what may.

A Journey in Moonlit Paths

The moonlight whispers soft and low,
It leads me where the shadows go.
Each step I take, a dream unfolds,
In silver beams, the night beholds.

Through trees that dance with gentle sway,
I chase the stars that guide my way.
With every breath, the night I greet,
A journey made in night's retreat.

Sails of Serendipity

The winds of fate blow wild and free,
They carry hopes across the sea.
With sails that catch the dreams we weave,
In tides of chance, we dare believe.

Each wave a chance, each crest a call,
Together we will rise or fall.
In sunset's glow, our spirits soar,
Exploring shores we've yet to explore.

Guiding Light of Passions

A candle's flame, it flickers bright,
It guides us through the darkest night.
With passion's fire, our hearts ignite,
And shadows fade, giving us sight.

In every dream, a spark we find,
A guiding light that's intertwined.
With fervent hearts, we chase the day,
For passions lead us on our way.

Tapestry of Talents

In threads of skill, we intertwine,
Each unique color, a design.
With hands that craft and hearts that sing,
Together we create each thing.

A tapestry of dreams we weave,
In every stitch, we dare believe.
With woven hopes, we stand as one,
A masterpiece when day is done.

Beyond the Horizon

In the fading light, dreams take flight,
Waves whisper secrets of the night.
Stars emerge, one by one,
Guiding lost souls till the dawn has begun.

Mountains stand tall, touching the sky,
While the moon casts shadows, soft and shy.
Each breath is a promise, each heartbeat a song,
Beyond the horizon, where we all belong.

Echoes of Hope

In the silence of night, echoes resound,
Whispers of dreams, lost and found.
Each heartbeat a story, each tear a grace,
Together we rise, embracing the space.

With courage igniting the flame in our souls,
We gather our strength, we reclaim our roles.
Through storms and shadows, our spirits will soar,
Echoes of hope, forever we adore.

In Pursuit of Tomorrow

Chasing the dawn, with hearts open wide,
We dance with the future, our spirits untied.
Each step a promise, each glance a dream,
In pursuit of tomorrow, we follow the beam.

Through valleys of doubt, on mountains of light,
We carve out our paths, with courage in sight.
Hand in hand, we'll face the unknown,
In pursuit of tomorrow, we're never alone.

A Tapestry of Wishes

Threads of our hopes, woven in time,
Stitched with the laughter, and echoes of rhyme.
Each wish a color, bright and bold,
A tapestry crafted, our stories unfold.

In the loom of the universe, faith intertwines,
Binding our dreams, like delicate vines.
With every breath, new patterns we create,
A tapestry of wishes, forever innate.

A Journey to Wholeness

In the silence of dawn's embrace,
Footsteps echo nature's grace.
Finding pieces that once were lost,
Embracing change, no matter the cost.

Through valleys low and mountains tall,
Each struggle teaches, each stumble a call.
Building bridges from fear to trust,
In shadows found the light of must.

Whispers of the heart guide the way,
With every step, I learn to stay.
Fragments unite in a tapestry bright,
In the quest for wholeness, I find my light.

The Light of Endless Roads

Beneath the stars, the paths unfold,
Stories of journeys brave and bold.
Each road a chance, a turn to take,
In the night, a promise to make.

With lanterns lit by dreams we chase,
The road ahead a sacred space.
Guided by visions, we chase the dawn,
In the light of hope, we journey on.

The horizon beckons, wide and free,
A symphony of chance and destiny.
With every mile, the heart expands,
In the endless roads, we make our stands.

Midnight Musings of a Maker

In the quiet hush of night, I dwell,
Crafting stories only stars can tell.
Hands in motion, hearts ignited,
With shadows dancing, visions united.

Thoughts like paint on a canvas vast,
Moments captured, shadows cast.
The moon whispers secrets of creation,
In midnight musings, my inspiration.

With every stroke, a dream takes flight,
Breathing life into the still of night.
In the solitude, my spirit sings,
For I am maker of wondrous things.

Seeds of Inspiration

In the soil of thought, we plant our dreams,
Nurtured by light and silver beams.
Tiny whispers of what could grow,
In the heart's garden, passion flows.

Each idea a seed, so fragile and bright,
With care and courage, we give them light.
Through storms and sun, we hold them dear,
In the growth of our hopes, we conquer fear.

With hands outstretched, we nurture the earth,
Cherishing every moment, every birth.
Inspiration blooms where love is sown,
In the garden of life, we're never alone.

The Mirror of My Making

In the depths of silent night,
I gaze upon my soul's own light.
Reflections tell of joy and pain,
Each crack a tale, each flaw a gain.

Through the glass, I see my dreams,
Warped by life's unending schemes.
A tapestry of laugh and tear,
A journey shaped by hope and fear.

With every glance, I learn to be,
A stronger self, I strive to see.
The past may linger in its frame,
But in this mirror, I claim my name.

From fragments gathered, I stand tall,
Embracing beauties, flaws, and all.
In the mirror, I find the road,
A path that leads, a tale forebode.

Whispers of Ambition

In every heart, a quiet fire,
A song of hope, a bright desire.
Dreams dance on the edge of night,
Whispers urging me to take flight.

With every step, the shadows fade,
Each challenge met, a promise made.
Through valleys low and mountains high,
I rise anew, I dare to fly.

In the stillness, ambition breathes,
Tugging at the soul, it weaves.
A tapestry of goals and wants,
In every heartbeat, it conjures haunts.

Whispers echo, calling me near,
To chase the dreams I hold so dear.
With courage as my guiding light,
I'll seize the day, I'll dance through night.

Chasing Stardust

Underneath a velvet sky,
I reach for dreams that soar and fly.
Each twinkling light, a wish in flight,
Chasing stardust, through the night.

With every step upon the ground,
I seek the magic all around.
In moonlit paths, my heart takes flight,
Guided by the stars so bright.

The cosmos whispers secrets old,
Of adventures bold, of stories told.
I gather hope like grains of sand,
In this pursuit, I make my stand.

Every heartbeat fuels the chase,
A universe in endless space.
Through trails of light, I'll always roam,
In stardust dreams, I find my home.

Canvas of Aspirations

A canvas wide, with colors bright,
I paint my dreams, my heart's delight.
Each stroke a wish, a vivid hue,
A masterpiece I'll bring to view.

With brushes dipped in hope and care,
I blend the shadows, light, and dare.
Visions formed from the depths of mind,
In every layer, beauty's defined.

The palette sings of joy and woe,
Mixing thoughts like a ceaseless flow.
From sketches born, ambitions rise,
A vibrant world before my eyes.

In this creation, I find my voice,
In vibrant colors, I rejoice.
A canvas rich with dreams untold,
An artful life, a heart of gold.

The Heartbeat of Potential

In the hush of dawn's embrace,
Dreams awaken, softly trace.
Whispers dance on morning air,
Potential blooms, bright and rare.

With every step, a story unfolds,
In the heart, a fire that beholds.
Paths entwined, futures collide,
In each heartbeat, hope resides.

Through shadows cast and light so rare,
Courage finds a way to dare.
Echoes of the past might call,
But within us, we can stand tall.

Endless canvas, vibrant hue,
Creating life, old and new.
Steps we take, the journeys start,
With every beat, we shape our heart.

Labyrinths of Yearning

In twilight's glow, a maze we roam,
Seeking solace, far from home.
Walls of thought, they close in tight,
Yearning for love, for guiding light.

Each corner turned, a breath we take,
In silence deep, our hearts awake.
Longing whispers, shadows creep,
Promises made in dreams we keep.

Through intricate paths, hope sparks bright,
Navigating this endless night.
Every twist, each gentle curve,
Fuels the fire of what we serve.

Yet in this boundless web we hide,
Yearning voices swell with pride.
In the heart's core, the truth we find,
Labyrinths forged within the mind.

A Mosaic of Longing

Fragments of dreams upon the floor,
Each piece a tale, longing for more.
Colors blend and stories weave,
In the silence, we believe.

Artisans of heart and soul,
Every shard makes us whole.
Yearning hearts beneath the sky,
A mosaic formed by the why.

Textures tell of days gone past,
Moments fleeting, yet they last.
In the touch of cold and warm,
Longing shapes, a heartfelt charm.

When twilight falls and shadows dance,
In the pieces, find romance.
For every longing, there's a way,
A mosaic brightens the gray.

Flight of the Unseen

Amidst the clouds where whispers soar,
Unseen wings take flight, we explore.
Dreams aloft on gentle gales,
Invisible paths through secret trails.

In silent skies, we learn to glide,
With every hope, we turn the tide.
Voices carried on the breeze,
In surrender, we find our ease.

Hearts untethered, breaking free,
In the cosmos, we find our plea.
Every heartbeat, every sigh,
Guides the spirit as we fly.

Through the vast, eternal night,
The unseen dance ignites the light.
In this journey, souls embraced,
In freedom's song, we find our place.

Traces of a Vision

In shadows soft, a whisper gleams,
Fragments of light, elusive dreams.
Each step we take, a silent trace,
Of hopes that linger, time can't erase.

The world unfolds, a canvas bright,
With colors bold, in day and night.
Visions dance, like fireflies,
Guiding us through the vast, dark skies.

Moments fleeting, in memory's grip,
Woven tightly, on fate's long trip.
A tapestry of wishes spun,
In every heart, bright wishes run.

Yet in the quiet, we shall find,
The echoes of a heart aligned.
With every vision, we grow wise,
In the beauty of the softest skies.

Rise of the Adventurer

On mountains high, where eagles soar,
With winds that sing, adventures roar.
A heart once still, now starts to race,
With dreams to chase, and fears to face.

The road ahead, both wide and narrow,
Guided by stars, like a jolly sparrow.
With compass set, and spirit free,
We carve our path, just you and me.

Through forests dense, and rivers vast,
Each moment savored, none surpassed.
The thrill of life, in every stride,
In quest for truth, we shall abide.

Beneath the sun, or starlit skies,
The call of adventure never dies.
In every heartbeat, hear the call,
To rise and stand, and never fall.

The Echoing Call

In twilight hours, a voice does rise,
Echoing soft beneath the skies.
A call to hearts, both near and far,
To find the light, our guiding star.

In the silence, whispers bloom,
Awakening dreams that combat gloom.
Like a river's flow, it finds its way,
Through valleys deep, where shadows play.

Each note ascends, a timeless dance,
Inviting souls to take their chance.
The rhythm of life, in harmony,
Unites all hearts, sets spirits free.

So heed the call, in every song,
For in the echo, we all belong.
Together we'll rise, with courage tall,
Towards the dawn, heeding the call.

Notes from the Future

From tomorrow's edge, soft notes are sent,
Whispers of hope, on moments spent.
A melody from the unseen fate,
Guiding us gently, before it's late.

In pages blank, our stories wait,
To chart the course, and navigate.
With every choice, a line is drawn,
In the tapestry of a bright new dawn.

The future sings, a luring tune,
Framing dreams, like a silver moon.
With open hearts, we will aspire,
To write our notes, and never tire.

For in the threads of time's embrace,
We weave our tale, our rightful place.
In every note, a chance to learn,
From future's spark, we brightly burn.

The Spiral of Ambition

In shadows deep, our dreams ignite,
We climb the heights with all our might.
A whisper calls, the heart takes flight,
The spiral winds, a thrilling sight.

Through struggle's grasp, we carve our way,
Each step a choice, night turns to day.
With every fall, we learn to sway,
In this grand dance, we choose to play.

The peak may gleam, yet paths are fraught,
In twisted turns, we find our thought.
With visions clear, our battles fought,
The spiral leads to what we sought.

So rise, O soul, in your ascent,
Let doubt dissolve, become content.
For in ambition's sweet cement,
We find the path of true descent.

A Battle Against the Mundane

In every hour, the sameness creeps,
The clock ticks on as silence weeps.
Yet in the heart, a fire leaps,
To break the chains, to wake from sleeps.

With eyes alight, the mind will soar,
Defying all that's gone before.
We seek the new, we crave for more,
To paint the world with colors poor.

Through daily grind, we find our fight,
To spark the spark, to claim the light.
In battles fought, we find our right,
To break the mold, to take our flight.

Embrace the chaos, feel the rush,
In mundane's grip, we will not hush.
With every breath, we break the crush,
And in our hearts, the dream we hush.

Rising Sun of Opportunities

The dawn arrives with golden hue,
A canvas fresh, a world anew.
Each moment glows, a spark in view,
Inviting all to chase what's true.

With open hands, we reach for light,
The rising sun ignites the night.
In shadows passed, we find our sight,
And chase the dreams that feel just right.

Each path unfolds, a journey wide,
In every turn, there's hope inside.
With courage bold, we choose to ride,
Into the dawn, where dreams abide.

So let us stand as daybreak shines,
In every soul, a hope that twines.
For opportunities, like sun, aligns,
To cast away the dark confines.

Driven by Desire

In shadows deep, our hopes ignite,
We chase the stars, through endless night.
With every breath, a dream unfolds,
A fire within, our hearts behold.

Whispers of fate, they call our name,
Guiding us gently, through joy and pain.
Each step we take, a path we pave,
Fueled by the passion, that we crave.

In fierce pursuit, we run the race,
With courage bold, we find our place.
The world is vast, its beauty wide,
Driven by dreams, we turn the tide.

So let the flame light up the way,
For in our hearts, forever stay.
The spark of hope, the will to try,
Together we'll soar, beyond the sky.

The Heart's True Work

In silence deep, the heart does speak,
Its gentle words, not loud but meek.
Through trials faced, it finds its might,
A guiding force in darkest night.

With hands that touch, and eyes that see,
We build a world, where love is free.
Each act of grace, a tender glow,
In every heart, the seeds we sow.

In laughter shared, in tears we shed,
The heart's true work is never dead.
With every beat, it seeks to learn,
A flame of hope, forever burn.

Together we rise, through joy and strife,
The heart's true work, the gift of life.
In unity, we find our song,
The heart's sweet melody, where we belong.

Mosaics of Possibility

In broken pieces, beauty lies,
A tapestry, beneath the skies.
Each shard reflects a tale untold,
In every hue, a dream unfolds.

With colors bright, we patch the seams,
Creating worlds from hopeful dreams.
In every corner, magic waits,
Awakened hearts, defying fates.

Embrace the flaws, the twists of fate,
For in our hearts, we cultivate.
A canvas vast, where we can play,
Mosaics of hope, light up the way.

Together we build, with love and grace,
A brilliant dance, a warm embrace.
In every moment, a fresh design,
A tapestry of hearts, forever shine.

A Sky Full of Goals

Beneath the stars, our dreams take flight,
Soaring high, into the night.
With every wish, a spark ignites,
A galaxy of bold insights.

We trace the paths of hope and desire,
In every heart, a burning fire.
With courage strong, we face the storm,
In skies above, our spirits warm.

Through clouds that gather, we will rise,
With open hearts, and shining eyes.
For every setback, there's a way,
To reach the dawn, embrace the day.

A sky full of goals, awaits our hands,
Together we soar, across new lands.
In unity, our dreams unfold,
A future bright, a tale retold.

The Radiant Path

Beneath the sky, a journey begins,
Footprints laid with whispered dreams.
Sunlight dances on the gentle stream,
Guiding hearts where hope still wins.

Through the woods, a soft breeze sighs,
Echoes carrying the tales of old.
Each step forward, a bold surprise,
With every moment, courage unfolds.

Flowers bloom along the way,
Colors bright against the green.
Nature's canvas, bright and gay,
In its beauty, we are seen.

Boundless journeys, hand in hand,
Together chasing starlit nights.
On a radiant path, we stand,
Illuminated by shared lights.

The Beacon of Intent

A flicker warms the darkest night,
A candle's flame of purest thought.
In the silence, our hearts ignite,
With every wish, a lesson taught.

Across the waves, intentions soar,
Like ships that sail to distant shores.
With steadfast minds, we seek for more,
Each heartbeat whispers, adventure roars.

In the garden of our desires,
Seeds of purpose find their ground.
With nurturing hands, we stoke the fires,
In the light of intent, we are bound.

Through trials faced, we stay aligned,
The beacon's glow a guiding light.
Within our souls, a truth we find,
Together, we will take our flight.

Canvas of a Thousand Hues

Brush in hand, we paint our dreams,
Swirls of color, life anew.
Each stroke whispers with sunlit gleams,
Creating worlds, vibrant and true.

In every shade, a story breathes,
A tapestry of joy and pain.
From darkest nights, hope never leaves,
In our hearts, the lessons remain.

With splashes bold and gentle lines,
Visions mingle, dance, and flow.
In this art, our spirit shines,
A boundless realm where love can grow.

Together we weave the scenes,
A canvas bright, a shared delight.
In every hue, our life convenes,
Creating beauty, pure and bright.

The Thrill of the Pursuit

Chasing shadows in the light,
With every step, we feel alive.
Through the forest, a joyful flight,
It's in the journey, we truly thrive.

Mountains high and valleys low,
Uncharted paths beneath the sky.
With each breath, our passions glow,
In the chase, we learn to fly.

Time slips by, like grains of sand,
Yet we revel in every race.
Life's a tapestry, vast and grand,
In the pursuit, we find our place.

Together, hand in hand we run,
Hearts ablaze, our spirits free.
In this thrill, we've just begun,
The pursuit of dreams, you and me.

The Map of Aspirations

In dreams, we draw our paths anew,
With every line, we chase what's true.
Mountains high and valleys low,
Our hearts will guide where we must go.

Stars above, their light so bright,
Illuminating paths in the night.
With courage, we'll defy the storm,
A beacon of hope, we'll take our form.

Steps unwritten, journeys wide,
With hope as our ever-steady guide.
Beneath our feet, the soil is warm,
Together we'll rise, through any storm.

Journey through Infinite Landscapes

Across the fields of endless green,
Where dreams and wishes can be seen.
We wander through the golden light,
Chasing shadows, taking flight.

Mountains echo with our song,
The road is weary, but we are strong.
Every peak, a new surprise,
In the vastness, our spirit flies.

Through valleys deep and rivers wide,
We embrace the world, with hearts as guides.
With every step, new sights appear,
In infinite landscapes, we conquer fear.

The Colors of Determination

In shades of red, the fire ignites,
Passion burns through long, dark nights.
With every brush, we paint our fate,
Colors bright, we resonate.

Golden hues of dreams unfold,
With silver threads of stories told.
Through shadows black, we find the light,
In vibrant strokes, we take our flight.

Each color speaks, a voice unique,
The canvas of life is what we seek.
With hands outstretched, we grasp our dreams,
In the spectrum of hope, our spirit beams.

Foundations of a Future

Brick by brick, we build our ground,
In unity, our strength is found.
With every choice, we lay the stone,
Creating paths for seeds we've sown.

Dreams like roots spread far and wide,
In the soil of hope, we take our stride.
From humble starts, our vision grows,
In gardens rich, our purpose shows.

Together we rise, hand in hand,
Creating futures, strong and grand.
With every heartbeat, we will strive,
Building foundations where dreams can thrive.

Reflections of Potential

In quiet moments, dreams arise,
Awakening hope where silence lies.
Each thought a spark, a guiding flame,
To light the path, to claim a name.

With every step, we leave the dark,
Embracing shadows, we find our mark.
The journey's long, yet hearts remain,
Resilient spirits dance in rain.

The mirror shows both flaws and grace,
A canvas framed in time and space.
We paint our future, stroke by stroke,
With every heartbeat, dreams invoke.

In unity, we rise and climb,
A chorus formed, transcending time.
Reflections deep, in silence found,
Together, we shall break new ground.

Steps Towards Stardom

With every leap, we touch the sky,
Chasing dreams as stars go by.
Falling hard, yet learning fast,
Each moment counts, we make it last.

The stage is set, the lights aglow,
A chance to shine, to let it flow.
In courage found, we take a stand,
With echoes of the cheering hand.

Though doubt may rise like morning mist,
We find our way, we shall persist.
Each note we sing, each line we speak,
Creativity flows, a vibrant streak.

Step by step, we carve our fate,
In the spotlight, we resonate.
Towards stardom's reach, we embrace the art,
For dreams evolve, igniting the heart.

The Lure of the Lighthouse

A beacon shines on the stormy sea,
Guiding ships where they long to be.
In darkness deep, its glow reveals,
A promise kept, a fate that heals.

Waves may crash, and winds may roar,
Yet steadfast stands the lighthouse shore.
With every flicker, hope is born,
A shelter found, where souls adorn.

As sailors chase the distant light,
They find their way through endless night.
The whispering tides, the beckoning call,
Lead them home, where hearts enthrall.

In solitude, the keeper waits,
With stories rich of life's debates.
The lure of the lighthouse ever bright,
A guiding star in the canvas of night.

Castles Built in Air

In dreams we build where clouds align,
Castles float, in sunlight shine.
Each brick a wish, each wall a prayer,
In realms of hope, where few may dare.

Visions dance in the sky so high,
A tapestry woven, ambitions fly.
With every heartbeat, fate unfolds,
An echo sweet, a tale retold.

Though winds may shift and shadows fall,
We stand our ground, we hear the call.
To reach for more, to seek what's fair,
To live our truth, our dreams laid bare.

In laughter bright, our spirits soar,
Building castles, forevermore.
In boundless skies, we find our place,
A legacy forged, a warm embrace.

The Architect of My Fate

In shadows cast by dreams untold,
I fashion plans with hands of gold.
Each choice I make, a step in time,
An edifice of hope, sublime.

With every brick, a story laid,
The paths I've walked, the risks I've braved.
The architect of all I see,
Is none but me, is none but me.

Through storms that rage and skies that clear,
I carve a way, I face my fear.
A blueprint drawn with heart and mind,
In this vast space, my fate defined.

At every turn, a lesson learned,
With every loss, a fire burned.
With faith as mortar, courage as stone,
I build a future, I stand alone.

A Symphony of Desires

Whispers dance in twilight's hue,
Each heartbeat sings a melody true.
A symphony of dreams take flight,
In silent whispers of the night.

Notes of longing fill the air,
Rich with hope, devoid of care.
I chase the rhythms, soft and bold,
In every measure, stories told.

Harmonies that gently sway,
Guide my path, come what may.
Desires merge, a perfect blend,
In vibrant strokes, realities mend.

Together in this grand refrain,
I find my joy, I face my pain.
A song of life, forever shared,
In this symphony, I'm ensnared.

In Search of Purposeful Sunrises

Each morning brings a brand new light,
I seek the dawn, I chase the bright.
In hues of gold and softest pink,
I find the space to stop and think.

Purpose whispers with the breeze,
In tranquil moments, it aims to please.
The sun ascends, a silent guide,
Illuminates the paths I stride.

With every rise, a chance reborn,
To leave behind the shades of scorn.
I grasp the warmth, I breathe in deep,
In purposeful sunrises, my soul takes leap.

Adventure beckons from new heights,
With every dawn, a chance ignites.
In search of purpose, I will soar,
Embracing life, forevermore.

Beneath the Cloak of Possibility

Underneath the stars that gleam,
Lies a world of endless dream.
A cloak of shades, both rich and rare,
Wraps me in its tender care.

Possibilities wait, like seeds in soil,
Blossoming forth, through sweat and toil.
I gather strength from every breath,
In shadows deep, I dance with death.

With open arms, I greet the night,
In countless paths, I seek the light.
Beneath the cloak, my heart will leap,
Into the vastness, mine to keep.

The future whispers, brave and bold,
In every moment, stories unfold.
A journey woven through every thread,
Beneath this cloak, I am led.

The Compass of Conviction

In every heart, a flame does burn,
Guiding souls through night's long turn.
With steady hand, it points the way,
To dreams that dance in light of day.

With faith as strong as ancient roots,
It thrives among the quiet shoots.
When shadows whisper, doubt may rise,
But truth will shine, a bright sunrise.

Through storms of doubt, we'll boldly steer,
Our compass set, our path is clear.
Each step we take, a pledge to trust,
In purpose strong, a must for us.

So let it guide, with passion's zest,
Our hearts aligned, we'll face the test.
For in conviction's steady hold,
Lie stories waiting to be told.

The Embers of Endeavor

From ashes rise, the ember glows,
A spark ignites, the journey flows.
Through trials faced, we find our might,
In darkened paths, we seek the light.

With each small step, the fire grows,
In labor's grasp, our purpose shows.
The warmth we share, a guiding hand,
In unity, together, we stand.

Against the winds, we fan the flame,
Our dreams alive, we'll stake our claim.
For every choice, a chance to rise,
With courage deep, we aim for skies.

As embers dance, we forge ahead,
In passion's glow, our hearts are fed.
With every breath, we stoke the fire,
And in our hearts, a fierce desire.

Chasing the Unseen

Beyond the veil, where whispers play,
We chase the dreams that drift away.
Through misty clouds, we reach for stars,
Exploring realms, both near and far.

With open hearts, we roam the night,
In shadows deep, we seek the light.
The unseen calls, a siren's song,
In every pulse, we feel we belong.

Though paths may twist, and doubts may creep,
We ride the winds, our faith runs deep.
In silent quests, we learn to hear,
The truths concealed, so bright, so clear.

Together bound, we'll take the leap,
In search for treasures we must keep.
For in the chase, our spirits soar,
The unseen waits, we'll seek for more.

A Quest for the Extraordinary

With hearts ablaze, we set our sights,
On distant shores and wondrous heights.
In every dream, a chance to find,
The extraordinary and the divine.

Through valleys low and mountains tall,
We hear the call, we heed the thrall.
Each step we take, a story we weave,
In the tapestry of those who believe.

With courage strong, we venture forth,
In search of what ignites our worth.
With open minds, we break the mold,
In the quest for truths that are tailed in gold.

Embrace the thrill, let passion lead,
In every heart, a daring seed.
A quest unfolds, with grace and flair,
In the extraordinary, we find our rare.

Portraits of Possibility

In colors bright, dreams unfold,
With whispers soft, futures told.
Each brushstroke holds a silent prayer,
For those who dare to envision where.

The canvas waits, a blank expanse,
Inviting souls for a daring dance.
Every choice, a line to draw,
A testament to the hope we saw.

Through shadows cast, light will break,
Revealing paths we long to take.
In every heart, a story spins,
A portrait framed by the life within.

So greet the dawn with open eyes,
Embrace the dreams, the endless skies.
For in each moment, we create,
A masterpiece of love and fate.

Threads of Destiny

Woven tightly, threads so fine,
Intertwined, our fates align.
Each life a strand, both strong and weak,
In this vast tapestry, we seek.

The loom spins tales of joy and strife,
Binding each moment with breath of life.
Unknown hands weave day by day,
In the fabric of time, we find our way.

Colors clash, yet beauty grows,
In every tear, a story shows.
Threads of peace and threads of pain,
Embrace the chaos, break the chain.

Together we stitch, together we mend,
Creating a future, round every bend.
For in these strands, we find our truth,
Eternal ties that carry our youth.

Wings of a Visionary

Soaring high on dreams unfurled,
A visionary sees the world.
With wings of hope, they glide and soar,
Opening hearts, a gentle roar.

They dance on air, defy the ground,
Where possibilities can be found.
Through clouds of doubt, their spirit shines,
A beacon bright in shifting lines.

With courage strong and eyes so clear,
They chase the whispers, draw them near.
In every challenge, they plant a seed,
A flight of faith, a heart's true creed.

So let us join their lofty flight,
Embrace the shadows, seek the light.
With wings of valor, hearts ablaze,
Together we'll sing through all our days.

A Voyage of the Heart

Through tempest tides and calmest seas,
A voyage starts with whispered pleas.
The heart an anchor, steady and true,
Guiding the way to what is new.

With sails of trust, we chart the course,
Embracing joy and sorrow's force.
In every wave, a lesson learned,
For every soul, a passion burned.

The stars our map, the moon our guide,
In unity, we set aside.
A journey shared, through thick and thin,
Together we'll find what lies within.

So embark with love, let courage steer,
Through uncharted waters, far and near.
For in this voyage, joys we'll find,
A treasure trove, a heart entwined.

The Sculptor's Dream

In shadows deep, a vision formed,
The marble waits, by dreams adorned.
Chisels spark with every strike,
A soul released, a breath, a life.

With hands so skilled, the stone will yield,
Revealing truths, in silence sealed.
From formless block to beauty bright,
The sculptor's heart in pure delight.

Each fragment speaks of timeless grace,
In every curve, a sacred space.
The dream unfolds, a tale untold,
In whispers soft, as art grows bold.

A masterpiece, the future gleams,
Crafted from hopes and fragile dreams.
The sculptor sighs, the work's complete,
In stillness found, the heart will beat.

Beyond the Periphery

A horizon calls, the wild unknown,
Where dreams are sown and shadows grown.
The edge of thought, a daring leap,
To venture forth, no time for sleep.

In realms uncharted, pathways twist,
With every step, persisting mist.
The mind expands, its limits break,
In silence heard, the future wakes.

With vision clear, the journey flows,
Past every fear, the courage grows.
Each moment sparks a brand new fire,
A quest for truth, a heart's desire.

Beyond the light, the stars invite,
To wander far, embrace the night.
Here in the dark, our spirits roam,
In endless search, we find our home.

Envisioning the Unimagined

In whispered thoughts, ideas bloom,
Where visions dance in twilight's room.
The canvas waits for brush to meet,
A world reborn, creation's beat.

What if the stars could sing and play?
What if the dawn could stretch and sway?
The boldest dreams ignite the mind,
In realms where truth and hope are twined.

Let colors flow, let shapes arise,
In every stroke, the heart complies.
Beyond the edge of what we know,
The unimagined starts to grow.

A journey forged in vivid hues,
With every glance, an ancient muse.
In fleeting moments, life will teach,
The magic dwells within our reach.

A Universe of Endeavors

In starlit skies, the wishes soar,
A universe beyond the shore.
Each flicker bold, a dream takes flight,
In endless night, we chase the light.

With every breath, new paths ignite,
The heartbeats echo, pure delight.
Across the vast, our spirits blend,
In timeless tales, where journeys send.

Adventures beckon, whispers call,
Through luck and skill, we rise, we fall.
The threads we weave, from dusk to dawn,
In every loss, a strength is drawn.

A cosmic dance, the stars align,
In unity, our souls will shine.
Together we'll create, explore,
A universe of dreams and more.

The Path Less Traveled

In shadows deep, where few have tread,
The whispers call, the heart is led.
Each step a choice, a dance with fate,
In silence found, I shall create.

With nature's guide, through tangled trees,
I carve my path with gentle ease.
Though storms may rage, and doubts arise,
I'll seek the light beyond the skies.

A journey marked by grace and strife,
Unfolding the tapestry of life.
With every turn, a lesson learned,
In the ember's glow, my spirit burned.

The road may twist, but steadfast I stand,
With courage firm and open hand.
For in the wild, my soul takes flight,
The path less traveled, my heart's delight.

Crafting a Life's Calling

With hands of toil and heart of fire,
I forge my dreams, I build my spire.
Each day a chance to shape my way,
In clay of moments, I shall play.

The whisper of fate calls me to rise,
To paint my canvas beneath the skies.
With passion's brush, I blend and weave,
In every hue, I learn to believe.

Through trials faced, my spirit grows,
In every challenge, wisdom flows.
I gather threads from each embrace,
To sew my purpose, find my place.

A life's calling, a melody sweet,
In every heartbeat, my journey's beat.
With dreams aligned and courage true,
I craft the life I'm meant to pursue.

Wings of Purpose

On gentle winds, my spirit soars,
With wings of purpose, life explores.
Above the clouds, where dreams ignite,
I chase the stars, embrace the light.

Through valleys deep and mountains high,
The horizon calls, I cannot shy.
Each beat of wing, a call to brave,
In every challenge, I find the wave.

With every flight, a story spun,
Of battles fought and victories won.
The air, alive with hope and grace,
In vast expanse, I find my place.

For purpose guides my wayward heart,
In every ending, a new start.
With wings wide spread, I freely glide,
In the dance of fate, I take the ride.

A Symphony of Desires

In quiet moments, desires hum,
A symphony of dreams to come.
With each note played, a yearning grows,
A melody where passion flows.

Voices blend in sweet collide,
Each wish a chord in heart's divide.
The rhythm swells, the pulse aligns,
In harmony, my spirit finds.

Through crescendos bold, I rise and fall,
In gentle whispers, I hear the call.
With every heartbeat, a passion's plea,
A song of life sings out of me.

As echoes linger in the air,
I chase the notes, I lay them bare.
This symphony of desires, so true,
In every heartbeat, I find the view.

Whispers of Aspiration

In the stillness of the night,
Dreams take flight, hearts ignite.
Voices murmur, soft and clear,
Fueling hope that conquers fear.

Winds of change begin to stir,
With each sigh, they softly blur.
A tapestry of silent vows,
Beneath the stars, the spirit bows.

Mountains rise, but we must climb,
One small step at a time.
Paths unseen will come to light,
Guided by our inner sight.

With every challenge that we face,
We shapes our dreams, we find our place.
Whispers echo, strong and true,
Aspiration lives in you.

The Canvas of Ambitions

A canvas wide, untouched, and blank,
Brushes poised, ready to prank.
Colors mix, wild dreams collide,
A masterpiece we cannot hide.

Strokes of hope in bold arcs soar,
Each line a tale, a wish to explore.
With every hue, aspirations swirl,
Inspires hearts around the world.

Shades of courage paint the way,
Chasing goals that greet the day.
Pastel hopes and vibrant schemes,
Filling the palette of our dreams.

Vision clear, we stand with pride,
With every effort, we will stride.
The canvas waits for us to share,
Our ambitions bright, beyond compare.

Chasing Starlit Vistas

Underneath a velvet sky,
Starlit dreams begin to fly.
Guided by the moon's soft glow,
Chasing vistas, spirits grow.

Fields of wonder lie ahead,
Each step forward, fears we shed.
Whispers of adventure call,
To explore the skies, to rise, to fall.

With each sparkle, hope ignites,
Illuminating shadowed nights.
The constellations sing our song,
Inviting us to dance along.

Hand in hand, we make our way,
Through the darkness, into day.
Chasing starlit dreams we weave,
In this magic, we believe.

The Path Less Walked

Through tangled woods and thorny trails,
The path less walked, where courage prevails.
Each twist and turn, a story told,
In every step, the brave, the bold.

Whispers echo from the trees,
Encouraging hearts with gentle breeze.
Guiding souls that seek the light,
Finding peace in the quiet night.

Footprints fade in shadows cast,
Yet the journey builds from moments past.
With every choice, a chance to grow,
Discovering truths we didn't know.

Upon this road, we learn to trust,
In every corner, wisdom's must.
The path less walked, though winding tight,
Leads to dreams that take their flight.

The Art of Fulfillment

In quiet moments, peace unfolds,
A canvas stretched with dreams untold.
Each brushstroke whispers, 'You are enough,'
In life's great tapestry, we weave our love.

The heart finds joy in simple things,
A child's laugh, the warmth spring brings.
With gratitude, our spirits soar,
In every heartbeat, we seek for more.

Embrace the journey, cherish the ride,
With open hearts, let hope be our guide.
The art of living, the joy we find,
In every moment, the soul aligned.

Let kindness flow and laughter reign,
In shared connections, we break the chain.
Together we rise, together we mend,
In fulfillment's dance, let our hearts blend.

Dreams Woven in Time

In twilight's glow, our wishes rise,
Like stars that dance in endless skies.
Threads of visions, soft and bright,
Woven with courage, they take flight.

The past holds tales of hope and sorrow,
In dreams, we weave a brighter tomorrow.
Each heartbeat anchors, a guiding light,
In the tapestry of life, dreams ignite.

We chase the dawn, the morning's grace,
In every dream, we find our place.
With faith as our compass, we wander far,
In the vast expanse, we shine like stars.

Embrace the whispers of heart's desire,
In dreams alive, we rise and inspire.
With every step on this winding road,
The fabric of time, our dreams bestowed.

The Quest for Meaning

In every question, a journey starts,
Seeking truth within our hearts.
The path is veiled, yet brightly lit,
In the silence, wisdom sits.

Through trials faced and lessons learned,\nThe fire of
spirit, forever burned.
In fleeting moments, clarity sings,
The quest for meaning in all small things.

To love and learn, to laugh and cry,
In every struggle, we reach for the sky.
With open minds, we wander wide,
The quest for meaning, a timeless tide.

In the embrace of night's gentle hand,
We find our ground in the shifting sand.
Together we rise, in purpose entwined,
In the quest for meaning, our souls aligned.

The Alchemy of Passion

In hearts ablaze, a fire ignites,
The alchemy of passion, taking flight.
With dreams like gold, we dare to chase,
Transforming struggle into grace.

The rhythm of life, a beating drum,
In each endeavor, we overcome.
With fervor fierce, we carve our way,
In passion's light, we seize the day.

Through trials faced, we find our voice,
In every choice, we make our choice.
With every heartbeat, we shape our fate,
In passion's dance, we resonate.

So let your spirit soar and rise,
In passion's glow, we touch the skies.
The alchemy of dreams, vast and wide,
In every moment, let love be our guide.

Twilight of Ambition

In the dusk of dreams we stand,
Chasing shadows with trembling hands.
Stars fade softly in the night,
Ambitions lost, yet hearts still fight.

The whispering winds of fate call,
Echoes of glory, we rise and fall.
Each step forward, a dance with doubt,
In twilight's glow, we seek a route.

Vows made in silence, now unspoken,
Hope like a thread, tangled and broken.
With every heartbeat, futures blend,
In twilight's embrace, we transcend.

So let us wander through this haze,
In the twilight, we find our ways.
Though ambitions fade in the dying light,
New dreams ignite with the coming night.

Sculpting a New Reality

With clay in hand, we shape our fate,
Molding visions, never too late.
The art of living, a canvas wide,
Each stroke a journey, a heartfelt guide.

In the forge of will, we find our strength,
Hammering dreams across great lengths.
Every challenge, a spark of light,
Reshape the shadows, embrace the fight.

Unraveling fears like threads of gold,
In this new world, we dare be bold.
With every breath, foundations shift,
Sculpting realities, our timeless gift.

So let us craft with passion's fire,
Design a future that takes us higher.
In hands that mold, and hearts that see,
Together we thrive, together we're free.

A Journey Beyond Limits

Step by step, the path unfolds,
Beyond the mountains, legends told.
Each mile a story, every turn a chance,
In the rhythm of life, we find our dance.

Through valleys deep and rivers wide,
We chase the sun, hearts open wide.
With every heartbeat, a call to roam,
In the distance, we find our home.

The sky's the limit, or so they say,
Yet here we soar, come what may.
With courage as our guiding star,
We'll go beyond, we'll reach afar.

So let us journey, hand in hand,
To places vast, to wonderland.
For beyond the limits, dreams await,
In this grand voyage, we create our fate.

The Mirror of Aspirations

In the glass, reflections play,
Hopes and dreams in bright array.
What do we see in the shining light?
A world of possibilities in sight.

Every glance reveals our soul,
With fragmented pieces, we become whole.
In the depths of the mirror, we gaze and dive,
Finding the reasons to strive and thrive.

Echoes of vision shimmer and gleam,
Illuminating our deepest dream.
With each whisper, ambitions grow,
In the mirror's truth, we learn to flow.

So let us cherish what we behold,
In the mirror, our stories unfold.
For every aspiration, a chance to shine,
In this reflective dance, we intertwine.

The Soundtrack of Striving

In echoes of footsteps, we chase our dreams,
Notes of determination flow through our seams.
Each heartbeat's rhythm, a pulse of our hopes,
With every setback, our spirit copes.

The symphony builds, crescendos and falls,
Through struggles and triumphs, we answer the calls.
Our voices united, a chorus so bright,
Together we wander, igniting the night.

Melodies linger, like whispers of fate,
Guiding our journey, through paths innate.
With every new chapter, the music flows on,
A soundtrack of striving, forever our song.

In the silence that follows, reflections appear,
Of moments once lived, of laughter and fear.
Yet in the stillness, the echoes remain,
The soundtrack of striving, our proud refrain.

Navigating the Stars

Beneath a blanket of shimmering skies,
We chart our course where the universe lies.
With constellations guiding our way,
Each twinkling light holds a promise to stay.

We sail on dreams through the cosmic expanse,
Each star a whisper, inviting a dance.
In the vastness of night, we find our own path,
With every new orbit, we harness the math.

Galaxies beckon, their stories unfold,
Of wanderers lost, and the brave and the bold.
In the map of the heavens, our fates intertwine,
Navigating the stars, our spirits align.

With stardust in our veins, we rise and we roam,
In the embrace of the cosmos, we find our true home.
Together we'll journey, hand in hand we will soar,
Navigating the stars, forever wanting more.

Flickers of Fate

In the quiet whispers of dusk and dawn,
Fate plays its hand, as shadows are drawn.
Each flame that flickers, a choice to ignite,
In the tapestry woven, we find our light.

Moments unfold like petals in bloom,
A dance with the universe, dispelling all gloom.
As paths intertwine, we question and seek,
In the flickers of fate, our futures speak.

Through trials and choices, a story we weave,
Each thread a reminder of all we believe.
In the weaving of time, our destinies blend,
Flickers of fate, as the shadows transcend.

With courage as fuel, we embrace what may come,
In the flickers of fate, we find our own drum.
Together we journey, through light and through shade,
Embracing the magic that life's choices made.

Echoes of Calling

In the quiet of night, a whisper emerges,
An echo of calling that gently encourages.
With hearts wide open, we listen and learn,
The voice of our purpose begins to discern.

Through valleys and mountains, we wander the trails,
Seeking the wisdom that never quite fails.
In the rhythm of life, we find our own ground,
With echoes of calling, our truth is profound.

In the laughter of friends and the silence of thought,
Residing in moments, we're all gently caught.
The pulse of existence, a symphony clear,
With echoes of calling, our vision draws near.

As stars light the heavens and dreams fill the air,
We heed the callings that lead us with care.
To follow our hearts, that sacred appeal,
In the echoes of calling, we learn how to feel.

The Canvas of Tomorrow

Upon the canvas, dreams take flight,
Brushstrokes of hope in the soft twilight.
Colors of passion, vivid and bright,
Painting a future where all feels right.

Every line carved from lessons learned,
From flickers of joy to bridges burned.
We sketch our paths, with hearts well turned,
In the palette of life, our spirits yearned.

With each new dawn, fresh shades appear,
Whispers of wishes, soft as a tear.
In the silence, the visions steer,
Guiding our way to what we hold dear.

So let the colors boldly blend,
A masterpiece forged, where journeys mend.
In the canvas of tomorrow, hearts extend,
To craft a world where love won't end.

The Horizon Beckons

Beyond the hills, the horizon glows,
A promise of paths where adventure flows.
With every sunset, the mystery grows,
In the arms of the dawn, excitement sows.

Whispers of wanderers fill the air,
Stories of places, beyond compare.
In shadows they left, their dreams laid bare,
A map of the heart, entwined with care.

As sails unfurl with the morning breeze,
Waves dance to tunes that echo with ease.
Eyes on the distance, we're longing to seize,
The treasures awaiting, our souls to please.

So onward we journey, with spirits allied,
The horizon awaits, our faithful guide.
In the dance of the stars, our hopes abide,
With courage and love, we take the ride.